Freshwater Literary Journal

2016

Freshwater Literary Journal

Freshwater Literary Journal is published annually by
Asnuntuck Community College. We review poetry,
fiction, and creative nonfiction. The upcoming reading
period will be August 15, 2016, to February 15, 2017.
Responses sent by the end of March 2017. Poetry: Three
poems maximum, up to 40 lines each. Prose (fiction or
creative nonfiction): One or multiple pieces up to 1,500
words total. No previously published material.
Simultaneous submissions considered. E-mail
submissions to Freshwater@acc.commnet.edu.

The 2016-17 Freshwater Writing Contest will focus on
fiction. The contest will be open to full- and part-time
undergraduate students enrolled during the 2016-17
academic year at Connecticut's community colleges and
public universities with an entry deadline of January 31,
2017. More information will be available in fall 2016 at
www.asnuntuck.edu/freshwater.

Please follow *Freshwater* on Facebook: FreshwaterACC;
Twitter: @freshwater_mag; and Tumbler: freshwatermag.

Table of Contents

2016 Freshwater Writing Contest

Judge's Commentary

Judging the 2016 Freshwater poetry contest was an honor and a difficult task. While I was privileged to read some of the best poetry written in college classes today, creating a lineup of "winning" poems forced me to pass up others that deserved merit.

As poets, we write for ourselves and our readers. Choosing the topic, language, and form are all individual choices that are never completely right or wrong. We hope our reader will become part of the poem with us, as we sacrifice many of our innermost feelings.

I can say without reserve that this was accomplished by the poets. With each poem, I wanted to *know* the poet, talk about what gave their poem life. My thoughts about their poems remained long after the reading was completed.

Elizabeth Szewczyk, 2016 Contest Judge

Note: Many thanks to the Asnuntuck Community College Foundation for funding the contest prize money.

2016 Winners:

First Prize: "Monday Morning Mass" by Rebecca Rubin
        (page 9)

This short, fifteen-line narrative poem took my breath away with its surprising ending. Rich language makes each word count, and alliteration and sensory language add to this masterful writing. The use of enjambment occurs at just the right moment, when the poet tells the reader about the hands she can't stop thinking about. From here, four lines to the conclusion, she expertly twists the entire message, and we understand that, regardless of her faith, she's condemning herself to hell for the love she feels for her best friend. The final line, so simple in syntax, is perfect when put in italics. As soon as I read this poem, I knew it was the winner.

Second Prize: "I Don't Want to be Pretty Anymore" by Madeline DelGreco (page 10)

The title of this poem made me curious—I wanted to know why! Taking the reader through three years in four stanzas, the poet's angst of wanting to be beautiful is felt through metaphor, repetition, and simple/complex sentences. The final stanza, where she changes her mind when it's too late, contains the tragic ending, and our curiosity of the title is answered. Written in repetitive verse of the first line, this poet's form reminded me of the great poet, Lucille Clifton.

Third Prize: "Sestina for My Grandfather Fazioli" by Ruth Pagano (page 12)

A sestina is one of the most difficult form poems to write, with its constant repetition of five end words. This poet does it well, playing with different styles of words. I loved the poem's story, full of humor and love. Who would think a poem about beans could be so rich in imagery and metaphor? Well done.

First Honorable Mention: "The 2015 Syrian Refugee Crisis" by Nathan Boutin (page 14)

This bold narrative, timely in today's world, combines horror and hope. The poet never sounds sullen or sentimental, using purposeful vocabulary to enhance his message. I loved the way the poet twisted the narrative in the sixth stanza to give his opinion. This was a difficult poem to read because of the subject matter, but I felt hopeful in light of the poet's end stanza.

Second Honorable Mention: "Leftover" by Julia Alexander (page 16)

"Leftover" is a unique narrative poem, where the poet speaks directly to the reader. The question at the end of the first stanza sets the tone for the next five. Rich in metaphors, the use of the albatross and the mention of "meeks' inheritance" allows a juxtaposition for the rest of the poem's images. Very neatly done.

Third Honorable Mention: "Working Hands" by Nathan Boutin (page 18)

Telling a tale about hands isn't easy but this poet does so with expertise and beauty. Moving from hands that are "claws" to "mangy things" and finally "make the world come alive," this poem brings a subject from ashes to beauty, as the reader imagines the poet's mother's hands in each setting, useful and needed. It's rare to be able to write so deftly.

First Prize

Rebecca Rubin

Monday Morning Mass

I used to close my eyes during Monday morning Mass,
The Jew in a Catholic school, a fraud,
Afraid that at any moment someone would stand up,
Point at me, *Blasphemy!*
But I loved Mass, with its melodies,
And soothing meditations, the priests triumphant bellows,
Like a war hero returning from battle,
As if god himself had come to tell us a story.
I never heard a word of the homily, too lost in my own
          thoughts
As I looked down at my best friend's hands next to mine.
Our Fathers spewed from my lips,
Meaningless to me,
Who kept thinking about his hands.
Shit, I'm going to hell.
But those hands.

Madeline DelGreco

I Don't Want to be Pretty Anymore

Before I got pretty
nobody wanted to stain my porcelain skin
with their blood soaked finger tips.
I am fifteen
with braces on my teeth
and baby fat on my body
lining my eyes with too much black
and pinching my extra skin
begging to one day be beautiful.

Before I got pretty
I didn't know how to play games
and manipulation was still a dirty word.
I am sixteen
still longing to be beautiful.
I just got my braces off
and an ignorant boy in my class
told me I was getting there
and I thanked him.

Before I got pretty
my body was never my main attraction
and I was never a bet.
I am seventeen
I've started smoking cigarettes
and losing all my baby weight
I had my first kiss that year
and then a little bit more

---

with a boy who didn't care
and never called me beautiful.

Before I got pretty
alcohol wasn't poured into my drinks
and boys never touched the swell of my back.
I am eighteen and drunk
no longer vowing to one day be beautiful.
A boy just lead me to his car
and when he laid me down on the backseat
he whispered,
"You're so pretty."

Ruth Pagano

Sestina for My Grandfather Fazioli
"Fagioli" in Italian is the word for beans.

At age fifteen, by boat he arrived in America.
The officer at Ellis Island wrote down Dominik Fazeole
really misspelling his name.
He worked for the railroad ordering beans
and supplies for the Chinese workers' kitchen.
He treated them all like his family.

He returned to Troy, New York to raise his family
after he married my grandmother who changed his name
back to the right Dominic Fazioli.
As a life insurance salesman he sat in many a kitchen
encouraging saving by those who just immigrated to
      America.
Then home to his wife's delicious fresh green beans.

My grandmother cooked long hours in her delicious
      smelling kitchen
to feed the hungry mouths of nine children in her familia,
They all ate the pasta and cannelloni beans;
they loved escarole, sausage, polenta and calzone by
      name.
But when they grew tired of the Pasta Fagioli
She made them their favorite, hot dogs of America.

The Christian Brothers called my brother Tom the red
          headed jelly bean,
With that carrot top you can't be a Fazioli
Teasing him about his name
He resented that they were insulting his family.
Like an Irish maid come over to America
Every afternoon they made him sweep the kitchen.

Weeks before our wedding, Matteo took me to the Italian
          Kitchen
when his parents came to America.
Clipped to the menu was a card saying Pasta Fagioli
"Ha," I said, "What a joke you are making of my name."
His mama said "Come to Rome on your honeymoon to
          meet the familia,
we will teach you how to make pasta and beans."

In California, we gathered for a family
reunion for the 90th birthday of my dad Chris Fazioli
fifty of us from eight states of America.
The dinner was formal but, of course, included beans.
For hours food flowed continuously from the kitchen
The T-shirt we each wore proclaimed our common name.

Every night around the table in our kitchen eating beans
          we sat as a family,
proud to be in America with a name like Fazioli.

First Honorable Mention

Nathan Boutin

The 2015 Syrian Refugee Crisis

Dad and I are having dinner,
Sitting across a round table
Chipped and splintered like salted back roads,
Plates heaping with 50-cent mac n' cheese,
Two lumps of frying pan hamburgers
Soaked in grease and ketchup.
We don't talk much.

The television flashes a report.
Syrian refugees cross borders,
Many borders, cross deserts,
Cross fields and the Atlantic,
Cross to the United States' doorstep,
Knocking and crying for help.

"Towelheads," dad mumbles. He growls
Of Muslims taking over the country,
Home-made bombs in garages,
Suicide vests exploding. He recites
How they attacked us on 9/11,
Wipes his graying mustaches,
Slams his hands to the table.

I stuff my mouth with beef
And look away.
I know Syrian refugees have
Nothing to do with 9/11.
I see them in camps, children

In loincloths begging for food
On a dusty sidewalk, adults
Carrying crying babies,
Homes destroyed by war.

Dad talks about his country
And slurps his Coke.
He talks. I listen.

I want to say he's wrong,
Say these people don't want
To highjack planes
And kill Americans,
I want to tell him
Muslims are not evil.

But this is his house.
There is only his truth.
So I cut my hamburger,
Fiddle with my macaroni,
And nod my head.

Julia Alexander

Leftover

Salt sticks to the tongue of this
gaping mouth. When you obsess
over reduction, it's hard to not
submit to the hunger, bite the apple,
let the juice drip down your chin. But,
how would you begin to wash away
the taste of resignation?

My palms are still stained
crimson from these acts of longing,
biting knuckles, squeezing lemon wedges
into diet soda, and running until the
pressure rips through the bottoms of
my shoes. Some things can't carry
this extra weight.

I have dreams about swimming in the ocean,
white birds overhead, the waves don't take me
down, but there's dirt in my mouth, drying teeth
and tongue as it expands. I forget
how to swallow or even spit, wake up choking,
and sweat all day.

See, the albatross brings good fortune,
if you keep her alive, but I'm not one to
accept help or charity, not from some squat
bird. I would have shot her down too,
let us all succumb to the lack, and I wouldn't even

mind carrying the extra weight
around my neck.

This must be what was meant
by the meeks' inheritance.
I can have the whole world,
if only it is cut into small enough pieces,

but I don't clear my plate.
I scrape the excess into the bin.
The juice runs.

Nathan Boutin

Working Hands

My mother's hands are callused,
Tough skin shields slivers of copper wire
Trapped in her flesh, the long mill days
Carried beneath her fingers like shrapnel.
Her hands are Polish, white half-moons,
Yet shadowed by machine grease,
And muddied as they delve deep
In autumn lilacs and sun-dried coleus.
She's got a beat up pair of claws, but
What woman's wouldn't from working
12-hour shifts, tending the vegetables,
Burning fingertips on Galumpkis and Kielbasa,
Dropping plates and gathering glass
Shards with an arthritic touch?

My mother's not ashamed to wear
Jewelry on those mangy things,
Tacky, oversized bracelets, golden rings,
And emerald-stoned trinkets.
She gilds her hands and paints nails blue
To highlight on experience,
Each valley of her skin aged, worn-in
With tradition and eroded by overtime.

I see her now, on an autumn afternoon,
Fringing the house with red impatiens,
Mulching the flowerbed, planting marigolds
By the porch, her palms intimate

With each earthen crevice. She looks at me,
Another of her creations, straw hat
Toppling over her head.
I do not help her.
My hands are too small,
Too soft, too young.
Only hands so rugged and worked
Can make the world come alive.

Julia Alexander

Dead Man's Float

Soaked through from the rain,
you abandon a cigarette on the porch,
just like a every conversations we left
soggy and half-smoked, not quite
resolved,
waiting in vain to be picked back
up again.

You press your hands into my skin,
nothing budges, nothing burns,
How far will I be from you? A few hours?
A hundred years?

A hand in the churchyard
pushes itself through the dirt,
and for the brief instant before it surfaced,
we didn't even know it was there.

Dennis Barone

Matters of Faith

I know what I heard; I know what I saw. After the race I walked into the grotto. It really is quite pretty, though this whole town is so picturesque as to be almost unnatural. I don't know why I parked so far away from the start, but I didn't mind jogging downhill after. And in the grotto of all things there was a pay-phone. So I called and said I'd be a while for I finished third master--pretty good I thought--and so I'd stay to pick-up my prize, two, as it turned out: a Timex sports watch and a rather large, weighty, and impressive sports medal. Vanities of vanity, those trinkets can't compare to what I saw as I wandered in the grotto. After I put the pay-phone back in its proper place, I proceeded to walk around. You may doubt or you may laugh, but it is true. I am not a religious man, perhaps not even especially spiritual, but as I gazed upon Christ on the cross I witnessed a most extraordinary sight. I saw the heartbeat. And I am just the first of many who visited afterwards and witnessed the same pulsing beat. This strange vision cannot be called a mirage of a tired runner, weary with the strained rhythms of his own pulsing heart or the heat of the late afternoon summer sun. They came not only from the monastery to see this spectacle but from the university, too, and science seemed defeated by the undeniable fact of all that the professors could see with their own eyes, touch with their own hands, and test with the many instruments at their disposal. Everything came up pulsing.

Ace Boggess

My Lunar Voice

if I hadn't seen the moon that night
full & dripping its juice like a chicken breast

aloft like a lemon lollipop on a stick
out the narrow strip of glass in my cell

if I hadn't sucked down all that black bile
of my fear long enough to look up once

I might have given up on words
surrendered them to my silence seething

like a great burr underneath my skin
its agonizing chiding *shut your mouth*

stop that humming live awhile in loneliness
without the companionship of a pen

between your fingers but I did &
there it was above the fenced-in wasteland

the highway beyond & miles of headstones
made from the shadows of pines

as if set in place on purpose
like a string around my finger

or the button on a voice recorder
urging *please press here*

Keven Casey

A Near Miss

The oak had grown divided over time,
split at its top. And when half of that "Y"
sheared away at last and fell in the night,
its branches caressing down the clapboards
on the other side of the bassinet,
its new leaves sighed at their poor fortune --
to cast be down from their place in heaven
by some knotted flaw of grain inscribed
within their acorn a hundred years before.

Sleeping through the commotion, we awoke
to its wreckage run aground on the yard,
sprawled and silent in its twigged rigor.
With its leaves now limp and the house left whole
by just a few feet, we were left wondering
how many seeds of the near misses and worse
that are set to befall our lives were sewed
long ago, our branches destined to entwine,
our roots already mingling, unseen.

Benjamin J. Chase

The Time of Thinking

By the time you think
your thought has passed

like this evening's
last line of sunlight,

already a memory
of its travels.

Rachel Crawford

vanishing point

limestone crumbles beneath our boots,
chalks its name on the silver slate of the canoe
we half carry, half drag down to the river's edge

we slide into the water, glide past trees
leaning silently into their reflections,
drift until the current takes us, carries us along

we look ahead and say nothing,
trailing behind us our steadily disappearing *v*

Jamie Crepeau

Torture Cubed

In a cubic equation, the gang
of x is gathered threefold
on one side of the parallel
lines. They stare and point

at the lonesome figure on the other
side. It will be referred to as y
because one might think, "Why me?"
as the alligator teeth of their greater

numbers cut through the lines
at a diagonal, a carefully graphed out
show of "strength" that rises on one
side while falling on

the other, down into a circular
pit where the skin is always
exposed to the continuous burn
of hydrochloric acid.

Joe Cuthbert

Isaac

Father is the Voice
that lives inside the mountain,
the sound of snapping wood,
the promise of descendants like stars
reflected in the long, sharp knife.
The knife that cuts. I am fire.

Father is the fire,
center of our camp, a low, cracked voice,
and on his belt the dangling knife,
stern as the thorny mountain
that blots out the sky full of stars.
He uncoils rough rope. I am wood.

Father is the wood
carried on my back for the fire
that licks at the diamond stars.
He speaks always to the iron Voice
echoing everywhere on the mountain.
He ties me with rope, and I submit. I am knife.

Father is the knife
that waits for dead wood,
heaped on the speaking mountain.
See him; he kneels by the fire,
listens again to the Voice.
Does father hear me? I am stars.

Father is the stars,
blank eyes that stare at the knife
in his trembling hand. The Voice
tells him to put me on the wood,
bring the hungry fire,
begin the sacrifice. I am mountain.

Father is the mountain,
that stabs the watcher stars.
Face lit red by the fire,
he stretches out the knife,
holds it to my neck. On the wood,
I close my eyes. I am voice.

I pray: Father mountain Break the knife.
Soothe the stars Scatter the wood.
Put out the fire Hush the Voice.

Barbara Daniels

Why Am I Blind?

The last words of my friend's mother
were "Oh shit." My mother's were
"You are forgiven" when Sandra

bumped her, changing her Depends,
doing the ritual turning. "Why
am I blind?" Mom had asked.

"Because you're dying," I'd said.
"Your senses are failing. But
I'm told you'll hear us till the end."

"How long will it take?" "You mean
till you die?" The doctors thought
one more day. When I asked Sandra

to sing for Mom, it was Amazing
Grace, a great rich river of sound
as if we were standing in church.

Mom slept then. Or seemed
to be sleeping. I touched her arm.
Sandra left the room sobbing.

Barbara Daniels

Tree of the Gods

Or so it's called—ailanthus—forgetting
that gods are prone to accidents,
the world awash with sticky liquid,
fog drop-curtained over the city
as if a sky god spilled beer.

The ailanthus grows six feet a year,
stretches up toward the dirtied dome
of the sky. In the tree of the gods
chickadees sing, but it's an invader,
crowding roadsides and empty lots.

An urban tree harbors inclusions
(nails, wires, clothes hooks)
so sawmills don't want it. Some
people call it the tree of hell,
hating its stinking blossoms.

They can't kill it, can't stop
its suckers from breaking pavement,
taking down walls. But after wars,
the ailanthus rises in rubble.
When its leaves open, it's spring.

Michael Estabrook

daydream

These days life has too many moving parts
daughter moving back home house needing repairs
yard a mess, diets, aching joints, money trouble
when all I want is to read some Byron and Tennyson
out back beneath the shade tree.

Jean Esteve

Cochlea

As the story goes

a fish not quick
gets knocked about
by fidgety, insistent seawater
again and again
as wont of wave
again against thin fish skin.

Thin fish skin
dented then
after years of such behavior
captured and pocketed the salty
brawls,
while tubes attuned
to pitch and roll
lengthened, cured around
old ocean's old soul
like a snail
yes, quite like a snail
that lies buried now in the depths of your ear

or so I hear.

Brian Fanelli

What Memories Remain

I'll remember this—
the clack of your boots on hardwood
as you strolled through art galleries,
cut through crowds, paused near a Matisse,
tilted your head to study the work,
or maybe I'll recall you kneeling
in a garden, lime-colored gloves over your hands,
a small hole in the thumb,
smell of Earth on your cheeks and clothes,
or maybe an image of you holding the cats,
hugging them to your chest.

How will you remember me?
Perhaps cycling next to you, pointing
at the weeping willow on Pierce,
geese honking along the river walk
and blue herons craning their necks near water.
Maybe you'll flip through pages of lines
penned and recited for you at my writing desk
some past summer afternoon,
when you looked up from sketching to listen,
and I kissed your palms,
blackened and smudged with Sharpie.

Time allows us to forget
thrown keys, late night spats,
all the reasons we needed to leave.
You said you'd remove photos of me from frames,
lock them in a box with the poems.
Is that how you'll remember me,

something to be tucked away?
Will you unlock that box on quiet nights,
when the silence of the house makes you ache?

Joseph Frare

Delivering the Peace

In the crowded city of Philadelphia lies the new home of a short and stocky middle-aged policeman, Michael Bates. He travels on foot to his new place of work, making large strides as he glances at his wristwatch. Ignorant of others and only concerned about his arrival to his new position as an officer in the Philadelphia police force, he does not take heed to pedestrians walking past him. He runs into a tall, slim young man, dropping his briefcase to the ground in the process. The young man wears a round commercial hat over his barely visible blonde hair. Bold, black writing that says "Juliano's Pizzeria" displays neatly on the front just above the hat's brim. He wears a white polo shirt with the same words on the top of his right breast, and he appears to be holding a large, square-shaped, leathered object in his hands. The pizza delivery man does not hesitate in the slightest when realizing that Officer Bates's briefcase breaks, and all the papers litter the street. The young man keeps his blemished face down at the pizza box and continues to walk forward while speaking to Officer Bates in a rushed voice.

"Excuse me sir, I'm in a hurry."

Officer Bates becomes angered by him, and grabs the teenager by the collar. "Where the hell do you think you're going? I'm sure whoever's getting their lunch can wait a few minutes while you help me pick up these papers!"

The young man eyes Officer Bates for a brief second, showing a panicked expression. The kid appears very young, about seventeen or eighteen years old. The evidence? His red blemishes and few awkward facial hairs show that of a boy in the mid-process of puberty.

The kid turns his head away from Officer Bates, then violently breaks away and makes a run for it, continuing to his destination.

Officer Bates yells out to him, "That's fine then! Just leave! You don't want to miss out on a lousy two dollar tip!"

As the young delivery man leaves his sight, Officer Bates groans and begins cursing as he starts picking up papers.

"Pathetic! Such a stupid kid taking a worthless job too seriously."

Some papers blow onto a windshield of a moving car, and the vehicle spins momentarily out of control. Officer Bates sees this and quickly continues on with his large strides, only this time he goes much faster.
A long day passes, and the fall of night commences upon Philadelphia. Officer Bates makes it back to his elegant apartment on the third floor of a four-story building. The minute he walks through and slams the small door into the room, a feminine voice calls from further beyond and behind another door a few feet away from him. "Thank goodness you're home! I'm starving!"

Officer Bates's eyes widen, and he takes a gander at his phone. The handheld device points out that he has received two messages from his wife, telling him that there is no food in the house and that he must buy some. As soon as he looks away from his phone, his wife is standing a few feet in front of him. Her work clothes are partly undone, and her long brown curly hair is let wild. She notices no signs of food on her husband, and she raises her voice. "Where's the food!?" she asks desperately.

Officer Bates is startled by his wife's sudden

temper. It's been only two days since they moved into the city, and since then, they haven't been able to get groceries due to their busy work schedules. They usually go out to eat because they leave their jobs at the exact same time.

It just so happens that Officer Bates got out a bit late today, and it appears that the thought of food could no longer be clouded with the mindset of real estate duties for his wife.

"Why didn't you just get something to eat?" Officer Bates asks.

"I wanted to wait for you. Besides, I want to save myself a little bit of money."

The woman bends down, holding her stomach, and gives out a loud moan. Her long hair covers her smooth face, showing off the agony and only exposing her skinny shoulders positioned to keep those thin arms wrapped around her perfectly curved figure. Officer Bates becomes terrified. He has never experienced this before.

Is she pregnant? he thinks. *Is this a mood swing?* His questions are answered shortly. The woman's skin turns gray, and her eyes roll upward into her cranium. She bends backward, and her stomach starts to expand and take form like an alien symbiote in sci-fi movies. A tall, human-like creature emerges, still inside her stomach, and the woman's head and limbs are absorbed into the back of its deformed body.

Razor sharp claws, a very thin figure, black round eyes, and a large mouth with impaling teeth is in the presence of Officer Bates. A river of saliva flows around its teeth and pours down to the floor on the terrified husband's shoes.

"Yaah!" screams Officer Bates. He attempts to run out of the apartment, only to be cut in the back by the monster's sharp claws. His blood splatters across the room, and the officer falls on his stomach. He turns over and throws a loose lamp that has fallen on the floor near a small table. The monster catches it and devours it in one bite.

As Officer Bates prepares to endure a painful end, a loud scream echoes from the monster. Officer Bates eyes the abomination that was his wife and notices that a pizza cutter has impaled its left breast. A young man of average height and long black hair arrives next to him. He walks into the room as the monster backs off and takes out the steel cutter from its chest.

The kid looks to be in his early twenties, and has a face so chiseled and smooth you could say it was one of Michelangelo's works. The dashing young man wears a familiarly loose, white commercial short sleeve polo shirt over his lean build. In contrast to the attire of the blonde Bates had seen earlier, this kid has on a pair of light blue jeans that look worn and faded and only wrinkled at the bottom where they rest over his small dark sneakers. He wears that familiar white pizza hat with the restaurant name "Juliano's Pizzeria" on it, as well as what appears to be a utility belt containing a large pizza knife and a highly advanced, futuristic pizza cutter.

He also has a large, leather, strap-on pizza box, and is wearing it like a backpack. After his prodigious entrance, he shifts his clouded blue eyes to Officer Bates and calmly says, "The pizza's here."

Officer Bates is dumbfounded.

"I ... I didn't order ..."

The monster lunges at the pizza man, winding up its sharp, piercing, needle-like claws and anticipating the strike. The pizza man instinctively pulls out the large knife from his tight, black, leather sheath on his belt, and the monster's claws bounce off it upon impact. The pizza man runs at the monster with his knife and cuts off one of its arms in one fast swipe of the blade.

Dry crimson blood oozes from the creatures armless socket, and it releases another loud cry. The pizza man takes out a steel medieval gauntlet from his belt. He latches it on, checks the tightness of the steel glove on his left hand, and extends it down to almost the elbow.

"It's time to make a delivery."

With that, he opens up his box and pulls out a cheesy, square-shaped slice of pizza with his gauntlet hand. The meal still produces steam and is decorated with thin red pepperonis coated all over the top of its tender cheesy exterior. He lunges at the monster's head and shoves the pizza inside its mouth, as if throwing a hard punch.

The sound of teeth shattering and choking spreads throughout the entire building. Physical struggling and a strong silence take over for a while, and then a loud gulp. The creature returns back into the stomach of the middle-aged woman, and her body bends back upright. She soon falls to the floor, her arm intact and fast asleep as if having a pleasant dream. The pizza man walks towards a traumatized Officer Bates.

"She was pretty hungry. Good thing I came in time."

Officer Bates moves his disturbed eyes to his sleeping wife. "What...what happened to her? What ... did you do!?"

"Dinner time is no time to miss, sir," the pizza man replies. "She was starving, and from what I just encountered, she must have missed lunch too."

Officer Bates is speechless. Never has he seen something like this before. The pizza man walks past him to the entrance.

"It was a good thing your neighbors heard your wife making a ruckus. Otherwise I wouldn't have come." He leaves the room and enters the hallway.

"Wait!" Officer Bates calls out. "What about me!?"

"The ambulance is on their way. I just deliver the food." He walks down the hallway.

Officer Bates looks at his sleeping wife, then thinks back to that blonde pizza delivery man that ran into him hours earlier.

"I hope he made it in time," he mutters to himself.

John Grey

The Internet Age Begins

Nobody goes door to door anymore.
Nobody drives through every small town in the state
with a suitcase full of samples
and a spiel drummed into him
by the fat guy at head office
with the taste for cheap cigars.

Hasn't been a one since they found Tom Herkel
in that motel outside Wichita,
flat on his back, unblinking eyes
staring at the ceiling's octopus-shaped water stain.
His tongue was the last to sprout
"You really need this cleanser."
His hands were the last to squeeze
that green liquid onto the brown patch on a rug.

Nobody drives a battered Ford,
thinking "Today's the day, I make
my biggest sale ever."
Nobody, late at night,
pulls over into the parking lot
of a cheap motel,
barely enough strength left
to curse what a man must do
to make a living.

The maid found him.
She had no clue he was the last.
She just figured him for the latest.

Taylor Graham

Crossing

That dog you found dead
in the road, eyes open, blind to you;
eyes turned away, and up,
consumed—no, poured full of light;
risen-away from the last sip
of thirst. A shepherd-dog run out
of time. No crevice to crawl
into, just a stretch of asphalt.
You couldn't stop talking
about his eyes, asking if you dared
say God was inscribed in reverse
on his retina. Or some other
dumb human joke.
How could dead eyes be so bright
beyond words?
How awkward your wondering
what ever to call it, whatever extra-
scientific or mythic faith out
of reason. We all want a verifiable
explanation. A dead dog
on centerline. I want to keep
that light in my eyes as I cross.

Laura B. Hayden

Excerpt from *Song to Marjorie: Woody Guthrie's 2nd
Wife and Life Companion*

Chapter One: "Rhythm"

When Marjorie Mazia first stepped into Woody Guthrie's
Greenwich Village apartment in 1941, it must have
seemed like a diamond being tossed into the rough. Two
diamonds, actually, for Marjorie joined her good friend
and fellow dancer Sophie Maslow on this cockamamie
mission – Sophie's idea—to couple modern dance with
Woody's popular *Dust Bowl Ballads*. They envisioned a
production with Woody singing and strumming his opus
of the migrant Okies' plight onstage, accompanying
Martha Graham dancers, the leading method in
contemporary dance then and now.

Like most Americans in the early 40s, the women
had been struck by the *Ballad's* two three-disc record
collections, still the most successful album Woody
produced in his lifetime. Through the tracts of the eleven
songs that touched America's soul, Woody sings the
stories of farmers, laborers, and the families he met on his
travels across the panhandles of Texas and Oklahoma and
parts of New Mexico, Colorado, and Kansas; folk who
had been forced into unbearable hardship and crime
against the forces of nature and man. These people,
moreover, symbolized the lives of hundreds of thousands
of Americans, who having lost the means to their "Do,
Re, Me," as Woody put it, left the Plains to head west,
looking for work and land.

Twenty-four-year-old Marjorie first heard *Dust
Bowl Ballads* at her sister's home in Missouri when the

album was released a year earlier. "Tom Joad," a two-part song which tells the story of the paroled Joad's odyssey home, just after he ". . . got loose from McAlester Pen / On a charge called homicide," moved Marjorie to tears. Even then she was curious about the man who could capture a family's multi-generational story so poignantly in only seventeen stanzas of traditional verse.

Sophie and Marjorie walked to the top floor of the 6th Avenue loft where Woody and his band, the Almanac Players, lived and held social gatherings known for a their blend of music, corny jokes, and philosophizing. Coined "hootenannies," these get-togethers ushered in a new concept on the urban music scene.

The two young women bore gifts of fruit and the hope of a collaboration that might take place in just a few days. Sophie had already danced to Woody's recordings of "So Long It's Been Good to Know You" and "Goin' Down the Road Feeling Bad," in a small dance group she formed in addition to her work with Graham. Her costumes were accessorized with aprons and cowboy hats to help portray the slice of rural America the songs depicted. The choreography suggested more of a barn dance than classic dance.

The two women at the door of the Lower East Side apartment expected to be greeted by a man who looked as strong and commanding as the songs on his *Dust Bowl Ballads* album. A kind of working class Abraham Lincoln. Instead they found themselves looking eye-to-eye with the slight, 5'6", 125 pound Woody standing across the threshold, more rooster-like than presidential in appearance. For Marjorie, it was love at first sight. Some say the same for the rooster.

Woody listened to Sophie's brainchild, his interest piqued by both the idea and the two women's good looks. An easy "Sure," rolled off his tongue. Yet it remained uncertain how a live performance of Woody's nasal and raspy delivery, along with his folksy pronunciations like "*home*-a-cide" instead of "homicide," would fare as accompaniment for avant-garde dancers on a New York City stage. On the plus side, both choreography and accompaniment promised to be radical: Woody's in the way his ballads and talking blues lyrics expressed empathy for the have-nots of America, guaranteed to stir anti-capitalist protests; the ladies in the way the Martha Graham dance method embraced physical tension (with oftentimes, writhing and rolling movement), emotional feeling, and social message instead of the romantic flow and fancy of traditional ballet.

The next day, being surrounded by a roomful of rehearsing dancers mesmerized Woody. He even began wishing he too could dance and swore he'd start exercising and quit drinking and smoking on the spot. Then he picked up his guitar. The differences between ballad singing and choreography became as apparent as an elitist versus populist agenda. While the dancers executed precise steps to exact rhythms, Woody would pause his guitar-playing measures longer than usual *here* and run right into other verses *there* without a taking a rest or breath. And he *never* played anything the same way twice.

"Why do you have to stop all the time," Sophie asked the folksinger after each do-over seemed to stray farther and farther away from the rendition she had heard on his album. As a dancer so committed to precise and carefully measured movement, she didn't realize she was expecting him to do the exact opposite of what any true, red-white-and-blue folksinger does – ad lib. "Dancers can't work like that," complained Sophie after watching her dancers collide and fall, due to his capricious accompaniment. "They have to do it exactly the same every time."

Woody replied, "If you're the same, the weather's different, and if the weather is the same, you breathe different, and if you breathe the same, you rest or pause different." He went on to explain, "If I want to take a breath between verses, I play a few extra chords. And if I forget lines and want to remember them, I play a few extra chords. Eventually he stormed, "And if I want to get up and leave town, I get up and leave town."

Most of Woody's biographers characterize this first rehearsal of folk song and modern dance as nothing short of a disaster. Family members, however, inspired by Marjorie's recollection of the day, see the lighter side to the ill-fated run-through, and the guiding characteristics of their family life together: humor and chaos.

So ended the first rehearsal, but not Sophie's quest: to have her group perform live onstage with Woody Guthrie. Sophie tweaked her vision and turned to Woody again. But this time in *Folksay*, her new more cheerful rendition, she would dance to a *recording* of two *Dust Bowl Ballads*. Woody, still, would take the stage, alongside another guitar-playing "narrator," dramatic balladeer Earl Robinson (known for writing the music to "Joe Hill"). The two men would mostly swap songs and corny stories, for as much as Woody had trouble playing a song the same way twice for a group of dancers, he was a shoo-in for getting repeated laughs from the way he and Earl bantered the likes of their down home repartee, night after night.

Earl: Rain much around here?
Woody: Naw ... s'dry the grasshoppers gotta

jump three times just to stay even.
Earl: Must get pretty cold in the winter.
Woody: Not so cold … but pretty damn cold.

Before long, Sophie and company all went around rehearsal mimicking, "Not so cold . . . but *pretty damn cold*," to crack up one another on the spot.

Droll comedy routines mastered, singing songs precisely the same way for the sake of synchronized stage performance, still challenged the folksinger. But Sophie knew who could fix the problem. She called on her partner Marjorie for assistance. Both women were a cut above the members of Martha Graham's renowned troupe, but for different reasons. While Sophie was making a name for herself as a dancer and choreographer, Marjorie was rising above the Graham standard as a dancer and teacher. Who better, then, to coach the unfettered improviser on how to sing consistently, especially since Marjorie remained fascinated by the man? This early partnership became the stuff of family legend says Nora Guthrie, recalling her mother's stories about teaching Woody a thing or two about a dancer's rhythm.

Like a patient teacher with a slow, but willing student, my mother worked with him that night. She created flash cards with numbers and beat and words written out which Woody would faithfully follow. He played along, enjoying the company of this pretty dancer, and fascinated by her ability to organize and direct him. No one else had come close.

During production Sophie, among others, began to notice how much time Woody and Marjorie were together, sometimes off on one side of the stage, other times, out of sight. Earl, who shared Woody's interest in pretty Marjorie along with their stage performance, felt jealous that Woody had beaten him to gaining the dancer's affections. Yet, unbeknownst to him, Earl really never had a chance. How could he when, months before he had even joined the troupe, Marjorie Mazia spied a scrawny, boyish Woody Guthrie through the open door of his 6th Avenue apartment and knew, right then and there, she was going to marry him.

There was just one hitch. Marjorie Mazia was already married.

Works Cited

Anderson, Jack. "Sophie Maslow, 95, Choreographer with a Populist Spirit." *New York Times*, Late Edition (East Coast) ed.: 0. Jun 27 2006. *ProQuest.* Web. 20 July 2014.

Commanday, Irma. "Marjorie Guthrie." *Jewish Women: A Comprehensive Historical Encyclopedia.* 1 March 2009. Jewish Women's Archive. http://jwa.org/encyclopedia/article/guthrie-marjorie. Web 02 July 2014.

Cray, Ed. *Ramblin' Man. The Life and Times of Woody Guthrie.* New York: W.W. Norton, 2004.

Guthrie, Nora. "Sophie Maslow and Woody Guthrie." MRZINE. 07 November 2006. http://mrzine.monthlyreview.org/2006/guthrie110 706.html. Web 02 July 2014.

Harris, Joanna Gewertz. "From Tenement to Theater: Jewish Women As Dance Pioneers: Helen Becker (Tamiris), Anna Sokolow . .." *Judiasm* 45.3 (1996): 259. *MasterFILE Premier. Web. 02 July 2014*

Klein, Joe. *Woody Guthrie: A Life.* New York: Dell Publishing, 1980.

Ruth Holzer

The Dancing Boy

He's five years old, or maybe six,
a gray rag wound around his head.
The man who holds the camera
has ordered him to dance
in the dusty village street.

He stamps his feet, a marionette
in heavy shoes that once belonged
to someone else, then he rocks from side
to side, struggling to please,
and when his dance is done, he will be shot.

Ruth Holzer

The Poet At One Hundred

Despite her best efforts,
she did grow fat and lazy
during the blurred decades,
but now she's getting very thin again.

She stayed more or less healthy
for her age, then less and less so.
The words dwindled to a dribble
before failing her completely.

Confusion kept her company,
and strangers that she had to pay. In pain,
she cried out for her mother, believing
there was someone left to worry where she was.

Susan Johnson

My Teeth, My Teeth

I wonder what the poor people are doing
dad would say as he pumped lake water
directly into a basin to shave his nubbly lip,
6 AM. Another day at the mill that coughed
out mercaptans the way he coughed asbestos
out of his lungs. See him as he cleans up after
breakfast, mistakenly throwing his false teeth
into the wood stove, plunging his bare hands
into the flames and running with that fiery ball,
yelling my teeth, my teeth, before pumping
more water onto the melted mass, ghoulish smile
all pink and black. And see him now as he heads
off to work insulation around sweating pipes,
his hollowed out cheeks like a sucker punched
fish, except he's already laughing, gumming
his lunch. At six years old, I liked to scare myself
by looking at the charred remains he kept in a jar
like pickles, like a punch line to some terrible joke,
like the memory we all have of waking to a world

Susan Johnson

The First Assembly of God

At the First Assembly Of God parishioners
wrestle with a scattering of donated parts.
The first god always jerry rigged: feathers,
toothpicks, paper mache. You got drift wood
you use drift wood grooved and worn, scraped
of bark, of any sign it was once a rough and twisted
thing. You want your god smooth, super glued.
Something that stands up to throngs. Have you
assembled your god today? Trees assemble
their gods from hurricane force winds. Rivers
from foxes running up hill. A baker's god
is assembled from yeast and air. A banker's
from shell middens. To assemble her own god
an artist cuts a thin slice of salami onto a thin
slice of paper, frames it and watches the fat
bleed into a sun whose halo grows and glows.
At the gallery reception people cut chunks
of more salami, wipe their fingers and drop
the napkins in the trash. Enough art for one
day. Enough assembling. Time to run naked
through a snow squall. Curl like a braided rug
before a fire. Listen to a four stroke down in
the harbor: intake, compression, charge, release.

Susan Johnson

The Worst Pothole Of All Time

The worst pothole of all time takes your breath away
and doesn't give it back, is home to subterranean fish,
a new species of eel. It speaks solely of hermeneutical
endeavors, says enlightenment is for others, longs to be
tonight's breaking news. TWPOAT gnaws your tires,
swallows your mother's buick whole. A connoisseur
of extreme temperature shifts, it double majors in uncivil
engineering and ancient infrastructural designs.
Its favorite movie is Jaws. The worst pothole of all time
craves sinkhole designation, promotes itself as a smooth
talking highway in online dating, says signs of aging
are not signs of decline. TWPOAT knows your bumper
sticker is a band-aid covering scabs of rust, that your
tail pipe is a loose tooth. It favors headlines that read:
No one was injured in the crash though two died.

Emma Jones

Heather

Heather was a witch but we all liked her.

It spread quickly around the school when she came in ninth grade.

"Hey, that Heather girl can turn apple juice into booze! Sweet!"

"She healed my cat's broken claw by talking to him in Latin. Don't know how it worked, but bless her."

Goddess. Angel. Magician. But what she called herself was witch, so that's who she became.

I passed her on my horse in the March of my sophomore year. She was standing on the side of the road wearing a denim jacket over a t-shirt with the UNICEF logo on it and a pair of athletic shorts. Her long, dark hair was in a braid that laid across her shoulder. Everyone was pale up in Idaho, but Heather was olive-skinned.

"You look nice," Heather called to me. I didn't really think I did. I'd been paying more attention to her clothes than mine, to be honest. My clothes were my mother's favorite: The big floppy sunhat with the with the yellow ribbon, the peach blouse, and the thick beige skirt down to my knees. I stopped Roll of Thunder, the big senile bay my parents had gifted me on my tenth birthday. "I've never seen someone ride a horse to school."

"Don't you know? They call me Pony. My folks own that big farm up on the end of town. I rode a horse before I could walk." I said it with some pride but sometimes I hated how I sounded just like I was from Idaho. Nobody wants to sound like they're from here.

"What's your real name?" Heather asked.

"Epona. Some Irish goddess. I dunno. Call me Pony."

"I like Epona," Heather said. "Could I come to school on your horse?"

"Sure." Roll of Thunder was big. But Heather touched his side and he seemed to look more alive than usual, a veil of glaze lifting off his eyes and his legs turning spry. She jumped onto his back easily. She didn't comment on how I'd rolled my skirt up to my waist and my stockings were clearly visible. Roll of Thunder moved compliantly when I touched him. "He likes you, Heather."

"I like him." She smiled the whole way through, but we didn't say a word to each other. Not even 'bye.'

I didn't see Heather again until Roll of Thunder died. He was old as hell, that horse. It was bound to happen someday. But when it did it was a big old rainy day and it seemed like a death day. I bet lots of people died that day. My brother Hunter was making me a poached egg on the stove when the doorbell screeched. I shouted "I'll get it!" and scrambled across the floor so nobody else got there before me.

The rain was pouring outside. Heather was in the doorway. I'd learned from the attendance list that her last name was Smith. She didn't look like a Smith. In the rain, she wasn't even the least bit wet. She wasn't wearing a raincoat or anything. There was this space were rain just...wasn't around her. It scared me a little, to be honest.

"Hi, Heather," I said. I knew why she'd come.

"I know your horse Roll of Thunder has died," she said softly. "I am here to release his soul to the earth."

"How do you do that?"

"It's a quick ceremony. I just need to be here to do it because this was where he was born."

I hollered to Hunter. "It's my friend Heather! She liked Rolly Polly and wants to pay respects!" He yelled back an okay. Ma and Dad were off on a trip to Portland at some college fair. They'd tried to drag poor Hunter to it but I'd made a big old show about not wanting to be alone so they let him stay.

Heather asked to see our garden. I just let her do her thing. I watched from inside the stable while she picked thyme and rosemary and horehound. She'd produced a basket out of nowhere. Her herbs weren't wet at all. I kept looking back at Rolly Polly's empty stall and wondering about death.

"Can I have a lock of your hair?"

"Why?"

"So he can remember you in the afterlife."

I didn't know if what she was saying was true, but I picked a red piece of hair off my head and handed it to her. She dropped it into her pile of herbs and took a lighter out of her pocket. She burned them in Rolly's hay and sang a song in a language I didn't know. Her voice was soft and high and rhythmic. Her eyes were closed the whole time.

When she was done I told her thank you, because I felt a lot better about Rolly. She said it was her pleasure. I invited her to have lunch with us, not just because it's what Ma would've wanted me to do. She made everything feel so much brighter.

"Heather, right?" Hunter asked when she sat down at our table. She nodded. "Hunter Cartwright," he said. He offered her his hand. She held it and a look of understanding passed across her face.

"It's alright that you dropped out of college, Hunter. If you love to farm you should pursue your passion. The person you love is still around. Be yourself. No one will judge. I'm a witch and they don't judge me."

She smiled at him, her slim shoulders engulfed in her long, black hair. I don't think I ever saw my big brother smile that wide or look so puzzled in his whole life.

He made her an egg like mine. When the sun comes out after it rains the earth looks like a battlefield after a war, the trees defiant in standing tall after being pelted with water and wind. Hunter sent me and Heather up to pick mulberries from the tree. As soon as the sun comes out there's no excuse to be sitting around, he said. Heather said that was right. When she held my hand walking up the hill I felt something go through me, like a little jolt that made me feel like I could've walked for miles.

It got a little colder when we went up the grassy hill with the mulberry grove on top. The grass was so long it tickled the sides of my legs, and the ground was cool and wet after the rain. Heather was barefoot. She was wearing a pair of athletic shorts and a long, plain t-shirt. I never would have admitted it in my life but I kept just *looking at her.* The curve of her legs, the thickness of her hair. She was Heather. You just couldn't keep your eyes off her.

When we got to the top Heather laid down on her back in the grass. "Come lay down here. The grass looks as tall as the Seattle Space Needle."

I laid down. "You ever been to the Space Needle?"

"I went in a dream once," she said. "Your parents seemed tense. Is there anything I can do to help?"

"They're going through a rough thing with Hunter. He doesn't want to go back to school and Ma really wants him to. I don't know. Ma wants me to meet a guy and get married and keep wearing her skirts and petticoats. Dad wants me to do better than Hunter, but not *too* good because I'm a farm girl. Sometimes I feel like me and Hunter are spoiled milk from Broulim's and my parents want the receipts.

"I see," Heather said. She didn't give that sad nod people usually give when you tell them something bad happened to you. What she said next was a statement, something I thought of like a prayer in the months that came afterwards. "I don't think everything is as bad as you think."

"How do you mean?"

"I just know that your family will be alright. Witchy sense, you know?"

I looked at her. Her eyes were this deep, icy blue. She was a girl like me and I know what the bible says, but she was a *witch,* God's word probably didn't even touch her. And looking at her right then I thought I would cry.

"I love you, Heather."

She just took my hand and I felt that spark go through me again, except this time it wasn't a jolt, it was this tingly feeling settling into my body. It was like kissing an electric socket. We laid there like that, hand in hand, for who knows how long. She told me she loved me too without saying anything at all.

Joshua Keegan

The Withered Iris

April 8th, 1864

   It was a day just like any other; the sun was peeking through from behind the clouds in narrow shards creating a pied landscape over the rural Louisiana moors. In those days, Jaina was but a girl, a girl full of laughter, naïvety, and sheer childlike simplicity. She could feel a light breeze coming ever so slightly from the east; and there she lay, in a field so tranquil and serene you could nearly hear the flapping of the wings on the birds overhead. She spent the majority of her days roaming in those fields, simply existing in an imaginary world all of her own. But, times had changed, and with each passing day, the time in her beloved sanctuary began to dwindle.

   "Come in now darlin'. The sun is starting to set."

   She could hear her mother's voice reverberate through the rolling hills. It seemed to her that the call came earlier each day. What little Jaina did not realize was that her mother had very good reason for shortening her play time. The war raged on. Jaina was fully aware that there was a war being fought, but her age limited her capacity to truly comprehend the severity of it. She had never witnessed a war, she was much too young for those types of things, and though her mother had informed her of the hard truth, mere words do not hold weight.

April 9th, 1864

   The next morning, Jaina was awoken at the crack of dawn when the noises began. Noises that she had never heard before. Crackling and booming emitting in a repetitive nature. The hills echoed a harshness that pierced her restful slumber.

Her mother rushed in and scooped her up all in one motion. "It is happenin' my dear. Come, we must go."

They saddled up the horses to the small carriage they had. The carriage was dark and damp; revealing the poor care it had been given. Behind them was a scene both disastrous and angelic at the same time. There was an intense light being emitted from behind the thicket of trees that served as the small prairie houses' boundary line. As this scene grew smaller on the horizon, a new one ahead was coming into focus. Jaina, still shaken from the scene and exhausted by the adrenaline rush, allowed sleep to consume her.

April 10th, 1864

This time when Jaina had awoken, the scene was entirely new. She realized that they had not traveled far because she herself had visited this field before. But now the scene was completely different from the days she spent in this field full of childlike imagination. She had viewed numerous makeshift tents littering the Pleasant Hill landscape. Under these tents, hundreds of men lie writhing in pain and agony. Swarming around were a cast of volunteer nurses with very seldom a professional doctor sprinkled in. She could not ignore the blood soaked grass, trampled flat. Any flower that might have been growing in the landing is either flattened or dead at this point. Jaina stood spellbound at the scene she was taking in, leaving no detailed uninspected. She surveyed the nurses, fluttering around, trying to attend to every man that was in need. Some followed the doctors, too frightened to do anything without the physician's orders, others were more experienced at this sort of thing. As she stood there, surveying the scene, something peculiar caught her eye. Far off in the distance, a figure hid, attempting to be concealed by the silhouette of a tree. This peaked her interest greatly and due to her innate curiosity, she went to investigate, she started with a slow trot, eventually breaking out into a canter. As she arrived at the scene, she was petrified. All of the color seemed to drain out of the world as she saw a man sitting on the ground with his back against a tree, his lower body concealed under the hiding of a blanket. In reality he was in his mid-forties, but his appearance hinted that he could have been thirty years older. His cheeks were sullen, deflated, and sunk inward, adding to the rest of the wrinkles and splotches of dirt that crowded his complexion. She examined the gentlemen from top to bottom. As she did this her eyes stopped on a pin he wore on the pocket of his jacket. It depicted an eagle, gracefully spreading its wings outward, clutching something in its feet. Jaina couldn't decipher what they were due to the wear and tear the pin had obviously seen.

"Good mornin' sir, are you... all right?" Jaina half muttered through her shy attitude and embarrassment now that she realized she had undoubtedly intruded on this man's privacy.

"Fine, my dear child, just fine," he said in a manner as if he were talking to someone at a cocktail party. "Aren't you a sweet thing for carin' 'bout me."

"My daddy told me to always offer a helping hand when it is needed," she said replied with proud conviction.

"And where is your daddy?" he inquired.

All of the sudden, her demeanor changed and she began to mumble, it was nearly inaudible, but she managed to croak out four simple words: "I do not know."

"Let me guess, did your daddy go to war?" he

speculated.

She nodded.

"Do not worry sweet flower, I am sure your daddy is a triumphant hero and is on his way home to see you right now," he reassured her in an attempt to give her hope.

At that moment, Jaina ran off, tears welling up in her eyes. The man sat there with no attempt to run after her.

April 11ᵗʰ, 1864

The next day Jaina went from her home, which her and her mother were allowed to return to, to the exact same spot where she had the previous day. She had spent the entire evening replaying the encounter with the mysterious man in the woods. She needed to know more about him. Who he was, what his life was, and what he current situation was to be sitting in the remnants of a battlefield. Once again the man was there, in the same exact position he had been.

"Well hello darlin', fancy seeing you again," he said in the flashy manner he seemed to always exhibit.

Jaina sat next to him and once again struck up a conversation. She listened carefully, transfixed by the stories he told her, soaking up every specific detail. She felt a sense of comfort in this man. In truth, the resemblance to her father was noticeable. Not so much in appearance, but due to the similar personalities, every now and then she would catch a glimpse of his face. Or what she could remember of it. He regaled her with heroic fables of how he saved towns, rescued damsels, and accomplished near herculean tasks. At the end of each day, Jaina would leave the gentleman with a singular iris she had picked from her mother's garden.

And at the end of every day the gentleman would

say, "My dear child, you are the light in my own darkness."

This exact process had happened for the next few days.

April 13th, 1864

On the fourth day, Jaina came home at the end of her day with tears in her eyes. She entered her small rural prairie home and was swarmed by a barrage of questions aimed at her. Jaina's mother was a caring women, intelligent, and very forceful, in times like these, she had to be. Her husband was off to war and she was to fend for herself and for her daughter.

"What's wrong baby?" Jaina's mother inquired with concern in her voice.

"He is mad at me," she uttered through quiet sobs.

"Who is?"

"The gentleman."

"What gentleman?" her mother said in an alarming tone.

Jaina proceeded to tell her mother the events of her past few days.

"He will not talk to me, he just stays there silent. I know why too." she said.

"Why darlin'?"

"I did not go see him yesterday. I was playing in the fields and I forgot to go visit him. And when I went today he was probably mad. That's why he is ignorin' me," she explained.

Jaina's mother demanded for her to reveal where this man is and eventually dragged it out of her. She then proceeded to grab her shawl and commanded her to stay put or she would receive a very severe punishment. Jaina's mother never reprimanded her, she never really had a need to. Jaina was such a good daughter, but the natural mother instinct emerged and she was now a lioness protecting her cub from the danger of the world. She moved quickly, saddling up the horses and riding away in a flash. The mother finally arrived to the place where her daughter directed her to and observed a scene like she had never seen before. There he was, an ashen figure, with a sunken face and dirt all over him. She easily saw what was going on, but she wanted to be sure. She tore the blanket that resided over the man's legs off. Dried blood had filled the underside of the blanket and it was clearly seen that the man's right leg was blown clear off. The bandages that were concealing the point of impact had evidently stopped the bleeding, but it could not stop the infection. What had been there in the place of where a leg should have been was a pile of twigs, rocks, and dirt, shaped to give off the form of the lower part of the leg. In the concealment of the blanket, it appeared the man retained all of his extremities. Just then, the mother had noticed something familiar. The gentleman was surrounded by some of the iris's that came from her own garden.

She took a deep breath and whispered aloud to herself "Oh, my sweet child."
The protectiveness wore off but the sadness sunk in.

The mother had returned, now in a solemn state. As she passed through the door, she heard Jaina exclaim, "I got it!"

"What?" she replied.

"I figured it out, he isn't mad at me, he couldn't be, he's just sleeping, that all it is, right mama?" she questioned.

She answered the only way she could: "That's right baby girl, that's right."

Haley Kierstead

Our Place

I was running. Running through an autumn wood just laced with the first snow. Clouds rolled in and became part of a thickening darkness in the sky above. The leaves crunched beneath my dashing boots. The air chilled my cheeks pink and gusts of wind blew my hair wild.

He won't find me there.

Limbs reached out to tear at my skirt. I dodged branches, hopped fallen trees, and darted around fox holes.

Almost there.

I scared a deer on my way there. She had stopped a moment to stare at me with her black unblinking eyes before disappearing quickly into the trees, not leaving one trace of her presence behind.

I'm here.

There stood the tallest and thickest tree in all of the forest. Its bark winding into the ground created big roots that sprawled out like spider legs. I placed my hand to the special part in the bark, the soft spot that soon gave into my hand, and let me open the secret entry. I pushed the bark back into place when I was on the other side, inside the tree. There before me was the carved staircase, made entirely from the insides of the tree. A scraped hollow tree that stood among the rest, looking just as alive.

I made my way up the stairs, my steps slowed now. When I reached the top, I took in the room before me. Very narrow, but not too narrow a room, with a tall ceiling that eventually led up into the top branches of the tree. A bookcase, a round wood table made from the stump of another tree, a little bench, and shelves that held a couple cans of food.

This is our place. He made this for me. He can be quite the artist sometimes. He made this for me, to protect me.

I didn't have much time. I peered through a hole in the bark that a wood pecker had conveniently made for me. I didn't see him yet, but he'd be here soon. I grabbed the cans of food off the shelves and placed them in my bag. *Just in case.*

I waited not too long before I heard the crunching of leaves outside. I looked. There he was. Standing at the base of the tree, very unaware that I was inside of it, panting, looking around, and wiping the sweat from his forehead.

I fooled you old man, I laughed to myself silently. *You can't hurt me here. Not here, this is our place.*

He stood there. Too long. Almost so long I thought he might know I was in here, and remember this place, but he didn't.

In fact, he found the secret entrance completely by accident. He had leaned against the spot, and it gave in, making him fall backwards into the inside of the tree. I didn't stay any longer to find out what he did next.

I bolted to the back of the room, hoping he'd be more entranced by the finding of our tree, rather than thinking I'd be in here. I pushed on the secret window. We had used this window to hunt together when I was younger. Now it was going to save my life.

I quickly climbed down the tree, with careful footing, just as we had practiced in case of a forest fire. I jumped down from the tree and took off. And I think that's when he reached the room and peered out the window, because sooner than I had hoped, he was back on my trail.

Here I was again. Running. Dodging. Escaping.

I know these woods, he doesn't. At least I don't think he would remember...

I came to a large rock. The rock jutted out the side of the forest, beneath it a fast flowing creek. I turned around.

Too late.

There he was. Standing before me. Holding a knife and a dark brown bottle.

"Dad please," I gasped. His pupils were so big, his eyes looked black; glossy, as if he had a different lens than everyone else. And he certainly did.

He spat. "I'm not your dad." He took a step forward, and with that, I a step back.

"Not anymore," I whimpered. Mom had told me before she died that when dad changes, to stay away. Sometimes he would be a good one, but a lot of times, he would be a bad one.

He lunged for me. I jumped back, and I jumped back far. Into the air, my feet lost everything beneath them, and soon, I was falling. Falling down. Down. I screamed. Shots of pain coursed through my body, my blood pumping ... out of me.

"He doesn't know what he's doing sweetie," I recalled my mother saying, "he doesn't remember when he blacks out like this ... I really wish he would see a doctor." She sighed warmly into my ear as she held me to her chest and rocked me in her arms, dad's shouts just outside the door.

Water frothed over the rock I now lay on, slapping me in the face repeatedly. I tried to move, but it was over, I knew that much. Just as I was about to lose all consciousness, I heard a little *clink clink* and the brown bottle came tumbling down. It rolled next to me. Through wet eyelashes I tried to look up as far as I could without moving. My dad was still there, but he was crying. Leaning over the rock that jutted out the edge of the wood. I think he woke up.

This was our place.

Kudzai Mahwite

Ain't No Wrong : True Wish For Hindsight

Ain't no ravage my body with foul concoction
Ain't no endure hot-blood lust
Ain't no pilfer inert or emotion
Ain't no transform life to dust.

And yet mercurial sun burn my skin
And yet hot-blood thoughts afflict me
And yet imprisonment to me akin
And yet eternal dread's cauldron within me.

Be it be Zeus fabricate for me?
Or birth's fusion now just culmination?
Be it be my decision it do render?
Or sorrowful fate with no mender?

Newborn cries be just for warmth
Yet cold be just and bold
Me doth wish had been foretold
So to make destiny pure gold.

Four limbed motion so small a world
Dust in attic like dust in Ant-Arctic
Psychic would I have loved
So that future I not be daft.

Big matured all seeing eyes
But surety truly soon dies
All just nine planets in vast galaxy
It doth seem that aspiration be fantasy.

Please keep heed my verse not for all and sundry
Some do rejoice without break of sweat
Yet some do break without rejoice but sweat.

Ultimately all do love
To wish and hope to be foretold.

Andrea Martineau

Perfumed Portraits

Lilacs along the back fence
weaving throughout the barricade
blocking out the cranky Rottweilers
and the deadbeat's dead grass
from view of her play time sanctuary.

Lilacs in plastic paint cups
lining the low classroom windows
gifts for her teacher
remnants of recess escapades.

Lilacs lining the edge of
the driveway, offering a scented
embrace after the first boy
broke her heart for the fourth time.

Lilacs along the valley park path
slightly wilted from the warm, hazy
Saskatchewan sun
freed from the confines of the branches
to become her amethyst crown.

Emily Matthews

we turn them

there was no dread, resurfacing.
the only insect in a child's cruel hands,
i amputated reasoning, disarmed, as the room stood
waist-deep
in sugared brine.
it concerned me last night
that dreams resemble this waking fog too well, too well.
it rattles the teeth, the ribs, the
awed and opalescent eyes caught up in starlight from
six thousand years ago,
and I wonder if this is how we live now,
emptying hearts into the same backwater alley, trying to
find our own amid the bleeding,
dissolving piles lit pinprick-white by lights one
supernova away from still being real,
so we turn them all to halogen.
our reality deforms to a crow's schizoid self-pecking in a
screen forever,
forever.
what is truth but the breaths of insects, of birds,
wings lost in corduroy pockets?
a cold sleep, the earth's sigh as it swallows another blue,
frail limb.

Ken Meisel

Statue

Statue of a weeping angel, wings opened wide,
feet planted in a stance of sudden landing,
immortalized here on this cold stone monument,
your mouth frozen in an astonished O –
as if you'd discovered that the fall from eternity,
here, in the spinout from cloudburst to ground,

is nothing compared to the sudden shock and glue
of gravity, sealing you here on to this tombstone:

I want to offer you this small sliver of orange –
I want to watch your bewildered thirsty mouth
close on the sliced tart and tang of a summer day

as mine, too, has learned to close itself on joy
and wonder, on this lemon, lime and tangerine,

as mine has learned to savor and to swallow
all these falling days imbued with hue and flavor.

I want to sit beneath you, here in your company,
as the songs of warblers, singing in the swamp rose
that's growing above this mushroom-stained lake,
orchestrate the sun's yellowed, buttery descent,

as the field daisies and bell flowers, climbing up
around your small, oyster-stained feet, tickle you,

and enchant you to the hypnotic allure of sensation,
to this fervent hallucination of sound and sense,

as this grandfather oak tree, towering above you
like a watchful guard, keeps its sturdy vigil on you.

How bright it must be for your exalted opened eyes
as sunset dances over coffin plots and graves,
as it is buried into the scarlet-orange gleam
beyond the pine trees of this blustery city road,

how frightening, how exhilarating, to be born awake.

Tom Montag

All the Birds

All the birds
come like sorrows.

They perch and sing
and wait for

light to falter.
Oh, the darkness,

they know it well.
And still they sing.

James B. Nicola

Barrow and Cart

The barrow that my father used to haul
grass, leaves, and loam, had one wheel in the center.
It looked like a giant's wheelbarrow. My cart
had two wheels, low to the ground, lower than me.
We poached bay sprigs from the forest—yes I helped—
and landscaped our suburban sandy tract
into a theme park of forsythia
edging the street, lilacs out back (he had
me stick the cuttings in the ground and count
to seven years—like clockwork, how they bloomed!)
and, making a margin along the garage, the laurels
which ignited, mystic pink, one week each spring.

We stowed our wheelbarrow in the garage
until we got a shed; then, in the shed.
My cart, already rusted, lived outdoors.

But summer days, weekends in spring and fall,
the barrow and the hand cart could be seen
in tandem being wheeled across the street,
squeaks and all, to the woods and back again.

One autumn, only the hand cart lugged the leaves.
That was the fall that seemed to take forever.

Today the cart lies out back by the wall
which used to brace the row of juniper,
now buried by a fallen wall of stones;
the mountain laurels have long been dug up;
the forsythia along the street are overgrown;

a chain fence cuts through the lilacs, higher than me;
and the giant barrow's nowhere. Somebody
unaware of the utility of a wheelbarrow,
a brother most likely, sold it at a yard sale
one year, one of the seasons I was away.

Rebecca Oet

Indian River Lake

"Let's go canoeing, you and I," you say,
handing me an oar.
You give yourself the big blue one and I get the one
         ended oar.
Where is its twin? I wonder.
Is it floating out there, in the cool green beyond,
with the heavy end dipping in the water?
Or is it underneath a pile of junk, silently awaiting it's
         discovery?
Or maybe even my paddle was just created that way,
         lopsided,
knowing it's missing something but not knowing what.
We paddle, unsteadily at first but gaining speed,
barreling through the water,
leaving "V"s in our wake. The sky is navy dark,
tinged with orange at the bottoms.
A gaggle of geese stare at us reproachfully, geeselings
         tucked into their feathers.
As soon as we pass by, they flap their wings,
splashing, and their young take off behind them,
already following in their footsteps.
The older ones bark at the youngers, honking in a
         language I can't understand.
We slip through a patch of lilies,
our boat hissing and purring as I grab one and pull it out
         of the water.
Its roots dangle at the bottom,
scrabbling furiously at the muck, almost desperately.
The white beauty opens its petals,
the orange inside shaking like jelly with

every movement, trembling.
I bring it up to my nose, and the sweet,
innocent smell greets me.
Smiling, I throw it back into the water
among the lily pads,
and we row off,
stars dripping from our oars.

Simon Perchik

Untitled

To warm this grave its wick
is lit the way a small stone
ignites the Earth with footsteps

brought here to become the glow
dirt breathes in, half harvest
half let go and though the night sky

no longer makes room
it still thickens –you gather
as if all stones are emptied

for their canary-in-the-mine wind
darkness alone can calm, turn back
and your arm at last on its side

folded over the other :ice
headed for winter, filled
without a past, without faces.

Richard King Perkins II

Anything but Free

Nothing should have happened
but when our legs brushed beneath chairs
it brought the latent resolve of our eyes together
and more.
There is nothing that could have contained
all that followed,
what could obscure such candescence—?
When you laid back
against a scattering of cushions
and showed yourself unreservedly
I recall the smallness of your frame
and the first notion
that I would die with you
a thousand years from now
and that it would occur
even though it shouldn't
because phantom spiders had bound
our legs together with the strength
of their inescapable silken chains
and we never thought
for a moment
we were anything
but free.

Terry Persun

Going

Spotted brown hands
hold to my wrinkled skin,
a soft cloth, suede fingers, a felt heart.

The tests come back today.
Both in our own worlds,
mine a sunny hillside, hers a quiet beach,

but not in summer's heat, in cool fog, early
morning. Aged like wine
or a good scotch—does it really matter?

All those trips, moves, children;
all those nights loving
in the ways we have learned from each other.

The tests no longer scare either of us,
both willing to go
as long as we get to hold hands.

Robert Rothman

This Garden not Eden

Oh how you take my shovel, resistant yet yielding, the
      hardened

weathered features breaking into smiling cheeks of plump
      clumps and clods. You are my love and curse.

I dig because I must. I penetrate and turn over because
      my mind is so aligned. I plant because without
      you I am sterile. I am grateful the Sun and Water
      were not taken in the Exile.

Upright and proud, I bend. Far above the ground, I am
      brought down. Abstracted, I am rescued in the
      mud of my making.

Your sturdy legs anchored, bent at the waist like a dancer,
      hair tousled in the breeze, sweat from face and
      neck running down in rills over chest to gut to the
      garden of desire, you are beautiful in the
      concentration of Work.

This is paradise, Here, the earth spaded and turned, the
      seed planted and fed, each day returning, never
      out of mind.

What miracle this green stem appearing, climbing into air
      with no visible support. I watch with you the
      thickening of vision into stalk. Why talk?

If Abandoned then explain this scent and form? If Alone
why do I dance as the branches bend and dip?

Garden, given as remembrance and spur. All isn't lost
wasn't lost in the great divide.

And at end of day, spent and resting as a plow, *by the
sweat of their brow,* Garden regained in the
Outside. Too tired to do anything but Be.

Rebecca Rubin

Stocking The Hot Dog Shelves After a Blizzard

The blood vessels that line his forehead
Bulge with perspiration.
His arms flail frantically, one over the other,
Left, right, left, right,
A small bead of sweat slithers past his thick brow,
down his left cheek,
and lands gracefully on the tile floor
tinted gray with salt and dirt fro bottoms of shoes.
He occasionally loses his balance and a package of
processed meat falls from his grasp and lands on the floor
to be picked up instantly and wiped of dirt and grime
as he finally takes a step back to inspect
the perfection he has created
of rows upon fully stocked rows of hotdogs,
and only then,
can he acknowledge his daughter
who has come to visit him at work.

Rachel Scrivano

Midnight Crawl Through the Forest of Forgotten Fruit

I never wore my new sneakers over your house
because your yard was littered with shit.
Sticks were always too weak
to scrape it off
so the smell lingered, trailing behind
like Pig Pen's cloud of dust.

But this time I wore sandals, exposing my toes
to the blood-sucking mosquitoes and tall grass
that hit my ankles, scratching them as we waited
to run for the forest of forgotten fruit.

A limb snapped off your tree from a lightning storm-
it was our only protection from the *other*
lurking somewhere behind the shedding shed;
white paint flecks fallen like snowflakes
between the covered truck and stoned pathway.

We waited for our neighbor's porch light to dim
before running to collect more ripe fruit
from the forest—our ammo—
hiding them beneath our shirts so the juice
oozed upon our skin, sticking to us
and staining the fabric.

We crouched behind the garage
with beer bellies
shinning a flashlight at bushes
whenever we heard a sound.
It was dark, but we weren't afraid.

___

It was dark, but the fruit—
were they mangos or avocados?
Those green grenades grasped
in our grips
just waiting
to be thrown.

Emily Shields

Photograph of Raphella, 1893

Atop my Mother's dresser,
You stand poised in a white button-up blouse,
Eyes shining through the filmy decay,
Hair bound tightly to your head,
A pale arm twined around velvet drapes,
By the window of a home where my mother remembers
Playing on the floor around your paisley skirt,
That same flowing cloth that met your shoes,
A smile on your porcelain face,
Not yet showing the youth that would drain
As the years would pass and you, Raphella,
Laboring in the tobacco fields during blistering summers,
While raising seven children in a home that my mother
        told me
Was made of macaroni boxes underneath the siding,
That youth that would fade from those dark eyes,
As would your Sicilian tongue,
And all the recipes you brought over from the old
        country,
Would dissolve in their inky script, their pages yellowing,
Even the memory of the fig trees in your backyard,
From which you picked one last sweet fruit,
Before you left for Ellis Island at seventeen,
Never to return,
Never to reclaim such youth.

Richard Smith

North Korean Night

If you were flying over North Korea
holding your guts together with both
hands, bleeding all over
the inside of your airplane,
which was bleeding it's guts
all over the North Korean landscape
what would you do ?
Probably the same thing I did,
just sit there and hope to hell
you don't bleed to death
before your airplane makes it to
some place safe, which it didn't,
luckily I got out of it alive.
The airplane died a slow lingering death,
flattening itself out in the scrub
brush and tall grasses, elephant grass
or whatever you call it.
In a situation like this
you have as much choice,
as an ice cube on
a hot blacktop pavement.
Thank God for helicopters, this one
was searching for another plane
reported down nearby, and saw us go in.

Robin Stratton

A Sign

I was sitting in a coffee shop with a friend telling her about a woman I know who for years has been visited by spirits both benevolent and malicious. One time, she was driving in a rainstorm, and her windshield wipers just stopped. She prayed for a miracle, and they started again. Another time, she came home to find her house was a mess. Nothing was where it belonged, and the children denied any responsibility for the disorder. One night, she prayed for a sign to let her know that everything was going to be okay. In the morning, she went to the kitchen, and there on the table was a piece of paper, and written on the paper was the symbol for infinity. When I told my friend this story, I drew the symbol for infinity on a napkin. When we got up to go, I left the napkin on the table so it could be a sign for someone else.

Emily Strauss

City Streets of Macao

I watch out for the very old
on these busy streets, that tiny
bent man or woman shuffling
with a cane impeding traffic,
the casino dealers scowling
behind her push to get by,
the grandmother flattened
to the wall stops, breathes hard
peers with slitted eyes nearly
shut, leans heavily, waits
for them to pass before
starting with tiny uncertain steps
intent on a goal only she knows—
a shop, baguette, two tomatoes
a bit of pork to carry home
her trip long and painful.
I stop and watch when they pause
make sure they aren't knocked
down in the crowd, their feet still
move, their basket still clings
to their hands, I sigh when
those elegant youths rush by
oblivious to the wizened crone
standing in their path
unaware of age creeping up
the grandmother without purpose
now eating soft rice, peering out
her window at motion beyond
her understanding, waiting
waiting.

Vladimir Swirynsky

Korea—Observation Post
for Glenn Eure

The ghost of it whimpered back last night
from a cold November 50 years ago."

Somehow you endure the *things
of this world*, the clearness of winter,
half-moon your only eyes.
Bless the good earth, the black
boot frozen hand sticking
up through the half-finished
grave like an apology.

The fingers curled, a cup holder
for your coffee, a distraction from
the imagined stray bullet
with your name etched on it.

I have talked to those
troubled souls, men who only nod their
heads, the broken English of silence
that's an outcry wanting to explain
what we can't begin to understand.

War is a dull knife,
the poetry of survival,
a rough draft of us on bended
knee prying open the secret
compartment of hell.

—

Elizabeth Szewczyk

In Search of Unicorns
   for Allison

This morning over coffee, I can't help
but notice how shiny and thick
your chestnut hair looks,
like the unicorn's mane you created
at three, her spiraled horn
a cerebellum of ideas.

Did you want to be her? Leave
everyday earth, gallop away
with your thoughts, effervescent
illuminations of childhood?

This was our favorite time,
head to hip, plunging paper
and pen to my breast,
your persistent voice spilling
words faster than my fingers
could dance across the width.

Today I reassure you, she's not lost,
just bound under a mattress or locked
in a chest, her cone of stories waiting.
Tilting toward your face, my hand
brushes your cheek, you clasp a pen,
sip your coffee, smile. The unicorn appears.

Elizabeth Szewczyk

Protector

The room was quiet, only soft breathing,
as my daughter lay upright on the table, a paper gown
hiding every part of her torso. The lights were low, as
when the sun moves into twilight, everyone a shadow,
waiting. Sliding a rounded bar onto my daughter's belly,
the doctor found her, lighting the screen in front of him.

Our breathing stopped. In its place, the whoosh, whoosh
underneath her skin, four chambers opening and closing
as we watched her for the first time, this child,
the size of a cantaloupe, perfect round body and head,
nose the size of my pinkie tip, sucking her fingers

like popsicles, lips full and bowed, bending legs and toes,
twirling like a prima ballerina inside her mother. I
        watched
my daughter, tears sliding from her eyes, and returned
to the night I first held her, wispy ebony hair and mottled
pink skin, the blue veins in her legs traceable, her fingers

long and pointed, splayed to catch air. I remember
the whole sight of her, counted her breaths, every eye
flutter, discovered the meaning of protection. Now she
watches her own daughter, covers her womb with her
        hand,
a circular rubbing through the screen, around her
        daughter's

back, head, legs. She whispers, *Hello Sweetheart*
and the baby somersaults, recognizes her mother's voice

as my daughter offers to turn on her side for the child's
comfort, to give her more room to twirl, anything so she will
know mother is here, watching, applauding, protecting.

Luis White

Nothing but a Stump

With a computer in front of him, there was still a blank project on the screen. Cigarette in one hand and a steamy cup of coffee in the other, this was his daily ritual for the early morning. Usually he has the most inspiration in the early morning, maybe from the nicotine and caffeine rush that you can only get from that first cup or smoke, but for the past two mornings, nothing. Not a single thought of what he could work and it began to frustrate him. This happened to him yesterday, but he thought that it was just a small creation block that he would get over, but unfortunately not.

He didn't have much time to actually work on his craft because he had to get ready for work soon. This passion-driven activity was not making him much money, even though he dreamed of it being his career every day. His job working as a dental assistant was getting old, but it was paying the bills. Frustration began to set in more when still nothing was coming out, so he had to get up from his computer and take a walk. Upon leaving the house, the cool, brisk morning stung his face. It was 6:45 in the morning now, so the sun was just barely starting to come up.

While lighting another cigarette, he started down a little path that lay just behind his house. The walk takes about ten minutes, so he knew he would have time when he got back to work on what he needed too. These walks usual bring inspiration either drum loops that he could create or melodies that could spark a whole new idea. Something complicated popped into his head, but complicated is what he enjoys.

When he finally got back to the house he went straight to his computer, tried to put this idea he got from the walk down, but failed. Must have been too complicated for him, and something inside didn't feel right. *Why try something complicated,* he thought. Maybe his personal life was getting in the way. It was 7:00 now; he was already stressed out, so he proceeded to light another cigarette, wishing in the back of his mind it were something else. *Not 'til after work,* he told himself. He got up from his computer, giving up for the time being. *Later on,* he told himself, knowing that maybe a beer would eliminate whatever problem was lingering deep inside.

Giving up was something he always thought about doing, thinking that maybe if he stopped his life might be a little less stressful. He pondered that thought, really thinking about what that meant. If he was stressed out from doing something that he supposedly enjoyed, how could he really enjoy it? When he first started making music, it was something he enjoyed, but as time went by, it started to become more of a hassle. It was something he was trying to force out. That must have been his problem. Forcing things out must take away his creativity to really get anything worthy for him to show off done.

His day at work went by fairly slow, as it usually does. Hearing the drill on people's teeth always played back in his brain. His lunch break was nothing special, and the tuna sandwich did not help with making it anymore better. When the day finally finished, he left to go back home.

The drive home was nothing special, and when he finally got home, he grabbed a beer and his bowl and started to relax. Sitting in front of his computer again for the second time today, he finally started to work. He never really knew why it was, but the weed and beer really helped with him being able to get his musical creativity out. However, usually there was a point when he couldn't really work anymore. Either he drank or smoked too much, which stopped him from being able to work more. When this came he just walked away. There must be a connection here. Waking up hung-over definitely did not help with him being able to work on his stuff in the morning. As he lay in bed, he thought he found his root cause for his block. Even though the weed and beer could help momentary, it was the reason why he couldn't work when he was sober. He closed his eyes. Morning would arrive again soon.

Margo Zeno

Bad Wizard

The wizard lived in a hill and he was wicked, or at least he should have been.

He ought to have lived in a tower, but the thought of so many stairs hurt his legs preemptively and the man who came round once a month asking for rent on the hill was easier to terrify than the sort of person who the wizard imagined would own a tower. The hill had been den to a lindworm once. It wasn't classically evil, but like him, it had a kind of charm.

He hadn't planned on being bad. It had been decided for him, with an apprenticeship to a lich at a young age. He'd never had the interest, really but wished he had. He tried his best to keep up the act but in his heart he knew otherwise.

The wizard was not wicked, you see, because despite his training towards the contrary, one day he met a hero and he did not want to kill him even a little bit.

The hero arrived one morning, on the closest thing the wizard had to a doorstep. He tromped all over the roof of the hill and caused dirt to shake down and then he stopped right in front of the entrance.

He had reddish hair cut bluntly to his collar, chain mail, snug hose, and high boots. He was built like a triangle balancing on one of its corners. When the wizard stuck his head out of the ground and hollered at him, his broad pleasant face transformed into a look of perfect alarm.

"What do you want!" the wizard hollered.

"I'm here to vanquish the wizard!" the hero shouted back. He was holding his sword over his head with both hands. "I hear he turns into a dragon! Very awful! What are you?"

"I'm the wizard!" He ducked, the sword nearly lopping off his topknot. "There's no dragon! Get lost!"

"No dragon?"

"Absolutely none!"

The hero set the point of his sword in the dirt and rested both hands on the hilt, and he chuckled. The chuckle turned anxious somewhere after the seventh or eighth "ha," and then the hero's legs went all slack and he sat in the grass, his sword in his lap. "I'm supposed to bring back your head."

The wizard's first instinct had been to call up all of the nearby ants to eat this man's eyes. But then he looked too closely at the hero's face and saw someone who was trying as hard as he was and having the same amount of success.

The wizard sighed heavily. "Let me check the bone pile."

The hero went to follow him down into the tunnel, and the wizard let him, but not before demanding, "Leave the sword outside."

Jamey was the hero's name. He had introduced himself as they crept down into the hill. He had not liked the beetles or the reptilian smell that the wizard had never been able to rid the hill of, but he did not mind having to sit on a rock with his elbows hitting his knees, or that the wizard put his feet on the table. He did not complain that the only sources of light were candles mashed into the walls and ceiling. Instead he peered around at all of the sundry instruments of bad wizardry: the crystals, the skulls, the blood and wax. He seemed impressed by these, and got up to touch most of them, poking and prodding and asking, "What does *this* do?"

The wizard was not used to visitors or people

talking to him or his things being rearranged. He knew a spell that would reduce a man's fingers to naught but bone and another to cause the tongue to drop from a person's head. But he cast neither, for Jamey was displaying the ghoulish enthusiasm that the wizard had never been able to muster, and this was as compelling as the urge for sacrifice you got on the eve of the Tatter Moon. That is to say, very.

Jamey examined the wizard's mirror with wide eyes. "Is this magic too?"

The mirror was stuck shoddily to the wall, and the wizard did not look in it often. He found this had a useful effect. If he didn't care enough to look at himself then he did not put in much effort to be the slightest bit neat or appealing. Wizards who were sinisterly polished looked like they had *ambition*. The wizard did not have ambition. He didn't know where you were supposed to get it. It was better to avoid the sun and wear a threadbare robe and pile his hair on top of his head to distract from the lack of beard. It was a good look, he thought—or well, a bad one. People were uncomfortable.

But Jamey was not. He was leaning in close and smiling, and this put the wizard off his guard.

"No," he told him.

Jamey gave the mirror a disappointed look. "Say, what is your name?"

"Elliot," said the wizard, and he went and dug through his bone collection so that he did not have to look at Jamey, whose eyes were intense.

"Elliot," asked Jamey. "Why are you helping me?"

Elliot set down the breastbone of a wren, and tossed a turtle shell over his shoulder. He'd have to reorganize *everything*. Meddling heroes. "So that you will leave me alone."

"Hmm," Jamey said, and there was something in his voice that made Elliot turn around. "I think that I won't."

He was examining a tiny bottle with unhealthy glee, and the sight of this caused Elliot to leap at him.

"That contains Duke Focalor the Drowner! Stop *touching* things!"

Jamey caught Elliot by the waist when he nearly fell.

"Sorry," he put the bottle gently in Elliot's hands. He steadied him. "I think that I am going to come back."

"*Why*?"

Jamey smiled again. He had dimples and almost all of his teeth. Elliot was charmed. He wondered if it showed. He didn't know what he was doing with his face.

"This hill is full of wonders!" Jamey cried, beaming. "And here you are, at the center!"

He took Elliot by the shoulders. "Apprentice me!"

Elliot could not speak for several minutes. He tried.

At last he said, "You have much to learn."

"I want to! Please!"

Elliot caught sight of a lizard's skull at the very bottom of the bone pile. He yanked it out and pressed into Jamey's hands. He kept his own there for a bit too long, and while Jamey did not seem to mind, Elliot flushed. He drew back, mumbled a quick glamour and flicked his wrist.

The skull transformed into a dragon's decapitated head, complete with oozing blood, trailing tendons, and a fly. Jamey let out a cry of delight.

Elliot bit back a grin. "Give that to whoever sent you, and we'll do lunch, to start. Wednesday."

Jamey was hefting the false head, admiring Elliot's spellwork and nodding. But as he heard the last bit, he frowned.

"Oh," he said. "Can't do Wednesday. Rescuing a damsel."

"Oh." Elliot felt as if something inside him had been squashed. Damsel! Damn it!

Jamey looked up at him. "I'm free Thursday."

Thursday?

"Thursday is good," Elliot said, glad for having the desolate social calendar of a hermit, even if the lifestyle was rapidly losing its appeal.

Jamey paused at the entrance to the hill, crouching with the false head snug in his brawny arms. "I can't even tell it's a spell! I can't wait to see—Elliot, you are a *marvel*!"

In his excitement he nearly fell, and when he caught himself, his face was very close to Elliot's. He looked like he wanted it to be closer.

Elliot raised a hand between them and grinned

"Don't rush things," he said, and realized he sounded playful. Jamey seemed to like it, for he was halfway down the road before he realized he'd forgotten his sword. Elliot was waiting for him.

"Uh," Jamey said, and then the chuckle from before came back.

Elliot handed him the weapon. He laughed too.

They stood, not exactly looking at each other for about a minute.

"Thursday!" both men cried, and then parted. As Elliot watched Jamey go, waving whenever he looked back, he thought that even if he didn't have the heart to be wicked, at least he had found someone who was willing to learn.

Contributors

Julia Alexander is an ex-college dropout, a friend to many dogs, and an avid watcher of *Keeping up with the Kardashians.* She founded *Insert Lit Mag Here,* and was its literary editor throughout its run in 2014. Subsequently, she founded Chipped Tooth Press, a small writing collective that seeks to instill a love of poetry in even the most relentless of naysayers, which she continues to head. Julia has published a handful of chapbooks and zines online, most notably, *A Collection of Bruises I Cannot Show Off, The Brake isn't on Your Side of the Car*, and *A Giant in this House.* Her first book of poetry, *The Dirt I Rise From,* was published by Paint Poetry Press in early 2015. She also has a full-length album of spoken work poetry, *Accepting the Facts* (2013). Currently, she is a student editor of *Freshwater Literary Journal* at Asnuntuck Community College, where she has dropped back into college to pursue an education in literature and creative writing.

Dennis Barone is the author of fourteen books and editor of seven, including *Garnet Poems: An Anthology of Connecticut Poetry Since 1776.* He is professor of English and American Studies at the University of Saint Joseph and the past Poet Laureate in West Hartford, Connecticut.

Ace Boggess is the author of two books of poetry: *The Prisoners* (Brick Road, 2014) and *The Beautiful Girl Whose Wish Was Not Fulfilled* (Highwire, 2003). His writing has appeared in *Harvard Review, Mid-American Review, RATTLE, River Styx*, and many other journals. He lives in Charleston, West Virginia.

Kevin Casey's work is forthcoming or has recently appeared in *Paper Nautilus, Rust + Moth, San Pedro River Review, decomP,* and other publications. His new chapbook *The Wind Considers Everything* was recently published by Flutter Press, and another from Red Dashboard is due out later this year. For more information, visit andwaking.com.

Nathan Boutin grew up in Plainfield, Connecticut and is currently enrolled at Eastern Connecticut State University as an English major with a minor in writing. He began writing in high school and was always drawn to his parents as natural subjects. They are simple, divorced people with low-wage jobs. While his never had much money during my childhood, he has always admired both of their determination with regards to work ethic and principled social etiquette. As such, he feels their hard work has greatly influenced his personal and professional life.

Benjamin J. Chase has published poems in several literary journals, including *Second Nature*, *The Helix*, *Fresh Ink*, *Christianity and Literature*, and *Windhover*. A Connecticut native, Ben teaches English at Christian Heritage High School and is currently working on an M.F.A. in Poetry at Western Connecticut State University.

Rachel Crawford's poetry appears in *The Lyric*, *Red Rock Review*, *Illya's Honey, Mudlark: An Online Journal of Poetry and Poetics*, *Lucid Rhythms*, *Apeiron Review*, *Figures of Speech*, *Yellow Chair Review*, *Anima Poetry Journal*, *RiverSedge*, *Rock & Sling: A Journal of Witness*, *Red River Review*, and *The Wayfarer: A Journal of Contemplative Literature*. Her short stories appear in *Crack the Spine Literary Magazine* and *Her Texas: Story, Image, Poem & Song* (of which she is contributing co-editor). She is a recipient of Baylor University's Poetry in the Arts award and Press Women of Texas's short story award. She holds degrees from The University of Texas at Austin and Baylor University, and she has worked as a waitress, bail bondswoman, high school English teacher, university English teacher, editor, and writer. She lives in central Texas with her husband and daughter.

Jamie Crepeau is a machinist for money and a poet for fun. In 2014 and 2015 he was a student editor at Freshwater, and in 2014 he was the recipient of Asnuntuck Community College's Excellence in Poetry Award. The guidance of instructors such as Edwina Trentham and Lisa Mangini helped him evolve from a good poet to an outstanding poet. He has spent so much time trying new things with his writing that he has forgotten where his comfort zone is. He has had poems published in Freshwater, Helix, Fresh Ink, and Crab Creek Review.

Joe Cuthbert enjoys experimenting with form and language. He writes anagram poems for fun and has been studying Welsh and Irish forms. His work as a technical writer enriches his poetry. His poetry has been published in the *Stillwater Review* and the South Mountain Poets Anthology: *Off Line*. He is the Treasurer of South Mountain Poets.

Barbara Daniels's book *Rose Fever: Poems* was published by WordTech Press and her chapbooks *Black Sails, Quinn & Marie,* and *Moon Kitchen* by Casa de Cinco Hermanas Press. Her poetry has appeared in

Prairie Schooner, WomenArts, Mid-American Review, The Literary Review, and many other journals. She received three Individual Artist Fellowships from the New Jersey State Council on the Arts.

Madeline DelGreco is a student at Eastern Connecticut State University who has been writing for as long as she can remember. When she was younger, she preferred short stories but developed a love affair with poetry as she matured. She uses writing as an outlet to express her scattered thoughts and feelings in an organized manner that people can understand. She just wishes to write something that people will find beautiful and carry with them for the rest of their lives.

Michael Estabrook is retired now, working around the yard, and writing more poems--or trying to anyhow.

Jean Esteve is a poet living in Oregon.

Brian Fanelli is the author of the chapbook *Front Man* (Big Table Publishing) and the full-length poetry collections *All That Remains* (Unbound Content) and *Waiting for the Dead to Speak* (forthcoming, fall 2016, NYQ Books). His poetry, essays, and book reviews have been published by *The Los Angeles Times, World Literature Today, The Paterson Literary Review, Kentucky Review, Main Street Rag,* and other publications. He has an M.F.A. from Wilkes University and a Ph.D. from Binghamton University. He is a professor of English at Lackawanna College.

Joseph Frare is an Asnuntuck Community College student living in Connecticut. This is his first publication and he looks forward to publishing more in the future. As of right now, his top two favorite hobbies are chopping down trees and dumping coal into trains. Writing follows closely behind as number three.

John Grey is an Australian poet and U.S. resident. He has recently published in *New Plains Review, Perceptions,* and *Sanskrit* and has work forthcoming in *South Carolina Review, Gargoyle, Owen Wister Review,* and *Louisiana Literature.*

Taylor Graham is a volunteer search-and-rescue dog handler in the Sierra Nevada. In addition to Freshwater, her poems are included in the anthologies *Villanelles* (Everyman's Library, 2012) and *California Poetry: From the Gold Rush to the Present* (Santa Clara University, 2004). Her latest book is *What the Wind Says* (Lummox Press, 2013), poems about living and working with her canine search partners over the past forty years.

Laura B, Hayden is the author of *Staying Alive: A Love Story,* a memoir. She is the 2016 recipient of the Eleventh Annual Woody Guthrie Fellowship, which will allow her to complete the biography *Song to Marjorie: Woody Guthrie's 2nd Wife and Life Companion.* Laura teaches writing at Asnuntuck Community College, in the Western Connecticut State University MFA in Creative and Professional Writing program, and at the Summer Medical and Dental Education Program at Yale.

Ruth Holzer's poetry has appeared previously in *Freshwater,* as well as in *California Quarterly, Connecticut River Review, Southern Poetry Review, Poet Lore, Blue Unicorn,* and many anthologies. A six-time Pushcart Prize nominee, she has published three chapbooks.

Susan Johnson has her M.F.A. and Ph.D. from the University of Massachusetts—Amherst where she teaches writing in the Isenberg School of Management. Her poems have recently appeared in *North American Review, Circe's Lament, The Kerf, Off The Coast, Helen, Comstock Review,* and *Bryant Literary Review.* Her chapbook *Impossible is Nothing* was published by Finishing Line Press.

Emma Jones is a part-time high school student and full-time writer from the neighborhood of Inwood in New York City, NY. She loves Stephen King, classic literature, and theatre of both musical and non-musical varieties. Emma was the 2015 recipient of the Paul Bloch Award for Creative Writing for an excerpt of her piece *Troubled Boys,* a novel about gay youth in 1920s New York. She participated in and completed NaNoWriMo in 2015. This is her first time publishing in a literary magazine.

Joshua Keegan is a dedicated perfectionist, a literary snob at heart, and a *Freshwater* literary editor. He is transferring to Central Connecticut State University for Public Relations and eventually plans to take over the world.

Haley Kierstead currently resides in the small town of Coxsackie, New York, with her boyfriend, Greg, and their three animals. She graduated from Asnuntuck Community College in 2015, and is now attending The College of Saint Rose in Albany, New York, to pursue her bachelor's degree in Industrial Organizational Psychology.

Joseph LeBlanc (cover photo) says, "The goal of all my photography is simple: to make people say 'Wow' and inspiring others to get out into the world and explore." Joseph is student at Asnuntuck Community College, and his photography can be found on Instagram @joe_leblancx.

Kudzai Mahwite is a young Zimbabwean poet inspired greatly by the works and life of William Shakespeare. He is an Economics student and as part of his studies runs a small-time blog on the African Economy. Kudzai is also a Sportswriter with Football.co.uk. You can follow him on Twitter @sir_tos.

Andrea Martineau is in her third year of study at the University of Regina completing a B.A. in English, a certificate in Public Relations, and a minor in Psychology. Aside from being a student, she is an intern at the Saskatchewan Book Awards and an editor at the *Road Maps & Life Rafts* literary magazine. She can usually be found devouring a novel, looking after her forest of houseplants, attending local writing events and workshops, or traveling about Canada.

Emily Matthews holds a B.A. in English and has been published in *Ant vs. Whale, Allegro Poetry,* and *Rebel 58 Magazine*. Her Cherokee roots draw her to write about nature in different, unexpected forms. She is also interested in cats, candles, and castles - in that order.

Ken Meisel is a poet and psychotherapist from the Detroit area. He is a 2012 Kresge Arts Literary Fellow, Pushcart Prize nominee, Swan Duckling chapbook contest winner, and author of six poetry collections: *The Drunken Sweetheart at My Door* (FutureCycle Press: 2015), *Scrap*

Metal Mantra Poems (Main Street Rag: 2013), *Beautiful Rust* (Bottom Dog Press: 2009), *Just Listening* (Pure Heart Press: 2007), *Before Exiting* (Pure Heart Press: 2006) and *Sometimes the Wind* (March Street Press: 2002). His work in over 80 national magazines including *Cream City Review, Rattle, Ruminate, Midwest Gothic, Concho River Review, San Pedro River Review, Boxcar Review, Birdfeast, Muddy River Poetry Review, Pirene's Fountain, Lake Effect, Third Wednesday and Bryant Literary Review.*

Tom Montag is most recently the author of *In This Place: Selected Poems 1982-2013.* He is a contributing writer at *Verse-Virtual* and in 2015 was the featured poet at *Atticus Review* (April) and *Contemporary American Voices* (August). Other poems are found at *Hamilton Stone Review, The Homestead Review, Little Patuxent Review, Mud Season Review, Poetry Quarterly, Provo Canyon Review, Third Wednesday,* and elsewhere.

Widely published on both sides of the Atlantic, James B. Nicola has several poetry awards and nominations to his credit, with recent poems in *Freshwater*, the *Southwest* and *Atlanta Reviews*, and *Rattle*. His nonfiction book, *Playing the Audience*, won a Choice award. His first full-length poetry collection, *Manhattan Plaza*, has just been released; his second, *Stage to Page: Poems from the Theater*, will be out in 2016. More at sites.google.com/site/jamesbnicola.

Rebecca Oet is a student from Solon, Ohio. She enjoys reading, writing short stories and poetry, and, of course, taking pictures. Rebecca is a national silver medalist in the 2015 Scholastic Art & Writing Awards and has won multiple awards for her writing and photography. She often fantasizes about growing wings and flying through the air. Ruth Pagano, MD, returned to community college to fill in gaps in her mostly scientific education in the 1960s with the ambition to cure cancer. After she retired from a career in medicine and health insurance business, she returned to take courses in early childhood education, sociology, psychology, culinary, and American literature. She loves the diversity of classmates particularly at Capital and Manchester Community Colleges.

Simon Perchik is an attorney whose poems have appeared in *Partisan Review, The Nation, Poetry, Osiris, The New Yorker*, and elsewhere. His most recent collection is *Almost Rain,* published by River Otter Press (2013). For more information, including free e-books, his essay titled "Magic, Illusion and Other Realities" please visit his website at www.simonperchik.com.

Richard King Perkins II is a state-sponsored advocate for residents in long-term care facilities. He lives in Crystal Lake, IL, USA with his wife, Vickie and daughter, Sage. He is a three-time Pushcart nominee and a Best of the Net nominee whose work has appeared in more than a thousand publications.

Terry Persun has published four poetry collections and six poetry chapbooks with small, independent publishers, and has published in *Wisconsin Review, Kansas Quarterly, NEBO, Bacopa*, and many others. He also writes novels in many genres, including historical fiction, mainstream, literary, and science fiction/fantasy. He is a Pushcart nominee, and has published technical articles in numerous engineering journals. His novel, *Cathedral of Dreams* is a *ForeWord* magazine Book of the Year finalist in the science fiction category. He has also been a finalist for the International Book Awards for his historical novel, *Ten Months in Wonderland* and his science fiction novel, *Hear No Evil*. His novel *Sweet Song* won a Silver IPPY Award. Terry's website is www.TerryPersun.com.

Robert Rothman lives in Northern California, near extensive trails and open space, with the Pacific Ocean over the hill. His work has appeared in the *Atlanta Review*, *The Alembic*, *Existere*, *the Meridian Anthology of Contemporary Poetry*, *Westview*, *Willow Review* and over twenty-five other literary journals. https://robertrothman.wordpress.com/

Rebecca Rubin is a senior English major and writing minor at Eastern Connecticut State University who one day hopes to be a professor of writing.

Rachel Scrivano is currently a junior at Eastern Connecticut State University, majoring in both Psychology and English. She has been writing since the third grade and still aspires to be an accomplished author.

Emily Shields is a senior at Eastern Connecticut State University majoring in Communications with minors in Writing and Psychology. She serves as the Opinion Editor for Eastern's newspaper, *Campus Lantern,* and was published in Eastern's 2014 literary journal, *Eastern Exposure.*

Robin Stratton has been a writing coach in the Boston area for over 20 years. She is the author of four novels, including one of which was a National Indie Excellence Book Award finalist, two collections of poetry and short fiction, and a writing guide. A four-time Pushcart Prize nominee, she's been published in *Word Riot, 63 Channels, Antithesis Common, Poor Richard's Almanac(k), Blink-Ink, Pig in a Poke, Chick Flicks, Up the Staircase, Shoots and Vines,* and many others. She is Acquisitions Editor for Big Table Publishing Company, Senior Editor of *Boston Literary Magazine,* and Director of the Newton Writing and Publishing Center.

Emily Strauss has an M.A. in English, but is self-taught in poetry, which she has written since college Over 300 of her poems appear in a wide variety of online venues and in anthologies, in the U.S. and abroad. The natural world is generally her framework; she also considers the stories of people and places around her. She is a semi-retired teacher living in California.

Vladimir Swirynsky's twenty-fourth book of poetry, *Sgt. Rock Chronicles*, has just been published by New Kiev Publishing. At 67 years of age, he is still excited about poetry.

Elizabeth Szewczyk is a recipient of the Connecticut Celebration of Excellence Award for writing, winner of the Manchester Community College poetry award, and the author of four books: *On Burying Moths and Calendars* (poetry), *This Becoming* (poetry), *My Bags Were Always Packed* (memoir) and *One Pound at a Time* (memoir). She is a past member of the editorial board of the literary journal *Freshwater*, and has taught writing, reading, and literature from middle school to college.

Luis White was on the editorial board of Freshwater in the fall of 2016 and graduated with a degree in Liberal Arts. He then transferred to Central Connecticut State University. This is his first published short story.

Margo Zeno is a writer and comic artist deeply influenced by fairy tales, the folk process, gruesome history, and subversive kindness. They are currently writing a novel that includes all of that, and are pursuing an undergraduate degree in English. You can find them on Twitter @margozeno, and their comic work at gumroad.com/margozeno.

31686766R00066

Made in the USA
Middletown, DE
08 May 2016